First World War
and Army of Occupation
War Diary
France, Belgium and Germany

20 DIVISION
Divisional Troops
Royal Army Medical Corps
Divisional Field Ambulance Workshop Unit
14 June 1915 - 31 March 1916

WO95/2110/1

The Naval & Military Press Ltd
www.nmarchive.com
Published in association with The National Archives

Published by

The Naval & Military Press Ltd

Unit 10 Ridgewood Industrial Park,

Uckfield, East Sussex,

TN22 5QE England

Tel: +44 (0) 1825 749494

www.naval-military-press.com

www.nmarchive.com

This diary has been reprinted in facsimile from the original. Any imperfections are inevitably reproduced and the quality may fall short of modern type and cartographic standards.

© **Crown Copyright**
Images reproduced by permission of The National Archives, London, England, 2015.

Contents

Document type	Place/Title	Date From	Date To
Heading	2110/1		
Heading	20th Division Fd Amb. Workshop Unit Jun 1915-Mar 1916		
Heading	20th Div June 1915 20th F.A.W.U. Vol I		
Heading	War Diary Of The 20th Divisional Ambulance Workshop from July 1915 to 31st January 1916		
War Diary	Grove Park	14/06/1915	21/06/1915
War Diary	Reading	22/06/1915	22/06/1915
War Diary	Devizes	22/06/1915	19/07/1915
War Diary	Avonmouth	19/06/1915	21/06/1915
War Diary	Southampton	21/06/1915	21/06/1915
War Diary	Havre	22/07/1915	22/07/1915
War Diary	Roven	22/07/1915	25/07/1915
War Diary	Neufchatel	25/07/1915	26/07/1915
War Diary	Abbeville	26/07/1915	26/07/1915
War Diary	St. Omer.	26/07/1915	27/07/1915
War Diary	St. Martin	27/07/1915	30/07/1915
War Diary	Merris	31/07/1915	24/08/1915
War Diary	Estaires	25/08/1915	27/01/1916
War Diary	Hazebrouck	27/01/1916	31/01/1916
Heading	War Diaries Of The 20th Divisional Field Ambulance Workshop Unit-Volumes 2 and 3. February and March 1916		
Heading	20 F.A.W.U. Roll 2, 3		
War Diary	Hazebrouck	01/02/1916	07/02/1916
War Diary	Esquel Becque	07/02/1916	13/02/1916
War Diary	St. Janter-Bierzen	13/02/1916	31/03/1916
Heading	R. Balfour Clarke Lt O.C. 20th Divl. Amb. Workshop		

20TH DIVISION

FD AMB. WORKSHOP UNIT
JUN 1915 - MAR 1916

20th F.A.U.
vol I

20th Div

F

June 1915
July
Aug
Sept
Oct
Nov
Dec

Confidential

War Diary
of the
20th Divisional Ambulance Workshop

from July 1915 to 31st January 1916

Army Form C. 2118.

WAR DIARY
INTELLIGENCE SUMMARY.
(Erase heading not required.)

Instructions regarding War Diaries and Intelligence Summaries are contained in F. S. Regs., Part II. and the Staff Manual respectively. Title pages will be prepared in manuscript.

Place	Date	Hour	Summary of Events and Information	Remarks and references to Appendices
GROVE PARK	June 14/6/15	10.0 AM	Posted O.C. F.A.W.U. 20th Div.	
"	15/6/15	-	Mobilised F.A.W.U., and 2nd Daimler Touring Car.	
"	16	10am	Took Stores in charge, collecting them from Woolwich, Shorts & others, and Woolwich.	
"	17	-		
"	18	-		War Office letter 96.20/A.S.0/805 addressed to M.G. I/c Administration I/c Command.
"	19	-	Preparing for 1st move — for DEVIZES. Received orders.	
"	20	-		
"	21	3.45pm	Left Grove Park with convoy (Unit complete) for DEVIZES via READING arriving at Reading 11.0 p.m. Parked and billeted there, personnel slept in vehicles.	
READING	22	12 noon	Overhauled Dudley. Deasy car, slight breakdown; renewed Petrol. Leaving READING 12 noon. Arrived DEVIZES, parked in Square, then Billeted in the Town. Self Billeted "BEAR" HOTEL.	
DEVIZES	"	7pm		
DEVIZES	26	9am	Moved convoy into field at "Hillworth"	
"	24	-	Moved my Billet to Private house (Fernleigh), Hillworth. Obtained and inspected cars. Reported to O.C., 265 Company, and was made a Temporary and Semi-attachment to this A.S.C. Company (2nd Div. Ammn. Column).	R.B.C. O.C. D.A.W.U.

Army Form C. 2118.

WAR DIARY
or
INTELLIGENCE SUMMARY.
(Erase heading not required.)

Instructions regarding War Diaries and Intelligence Summaries are contained in F. S. Regs., Part II. and the Staff Manual respectively. Title pages will be prepared in manuscript.

Place	Date	Hour	Summary of Events and Information	Remarks and references to Appendices
DEVIZES	JUNE 25		Started training self and newly built services, drill, and general discipline. Opened up 70 citolops and store bing. Made small running repairs on cars.	
"	26			
"	27			
"	28			
"	29		Men were inoculated, and granted 48 hrs. absence from duty.	
"	30			
"	JULY 1			
"	2		Continued training.	
"	3			
"	4			
"	5			
"	6	2 p.m.	Second Inoculation of Men, who were granted 48 hrs. absence [from duty].	
"	7		It was decided that we should go under canvas with the 268 Company in another part of the and larger field. Prepared lorry for this move.	
"	8			
"	9			
"	10		Moved to new field with 268 Company. Closed my billet and  went under canvas joining Officers Mess 268 Company.	R. B. L. Lr. OC D. A. W. V.

2353 Wt. W25111/1454 700,000 5/15 D. D. & L. A.D.S.S./Forms/C. 2118.

Army Form C. 2118.

WAR DIARY
or
INTELLIGENCE SUMMARY.
(Erase heading not required.)

Instructions regarding War Diaries and Intelligence Summaries are contained in F. S. Regs., Part II. and the Staff Manual respectively. Title pages will be prepared in manuscript.

Place	Date	Hour	Summary of Events and Information	Remarks and references to Appendices
	JULY			
DEVIZES	11		Continued previous training with the 268 Company, and started convoy practice.	
"	12	"		
"	13	"		
"	14	"		
"	15	"		
"	16	"		
"	17	"		
"	18	"		
	19	8 a.m.	Departed for Avonmouth via BATH and BRISTOL	
AVONMOUTH		3.15 p.m.	Arrived AVONMOUTH. Parked Convoy and billeted at Rest Camp. Reported to O.C., M.T. Depot.	
"	20	8 a.m.	Embarked Vehicles with 1 R.C.O. (Sgt. King) and 8 men who were temporarily attached for voyage to 18th Div. L.B. under its O.O.C., on S.S. "Jabra" from "S" Quay.	R.B.C. L-
"	21	4.30 a.m.	Self and Unit, minus 1 R.C.O. and 8 Men (previously embarked, on S.S. "Jabra"). Entrained for Southampton.	C.C.D.A.W.
SOUTHAMPTON	"	12 p.m.	Arrived at Southampton.	
"	"	8 p.m.	Embarked on "King Edward" for ROUEN.	

Army Form C. 2118.

WAR DIARY
or
INTELLIGENCE SUMMARY.
(Erase heading not required.)

Instructions regarding War Diaries and Intelligence Summaries are contained in F. S. Regs., Part II. and the Staff Manual respectively. Title pages will be prepared in manuscript.

Place	Date	Hour	Summary of Events and Information	Remarks and references to Appendices
	JULY			
HAVRE.	22	4 a.m.	Arrived at the mouth of the "Seine", safe journey, very crowded boat. No room for Officers to sleep.	
ROUEN.	"	9.30 a.m.	Paraded men for Medical Inspection. Billeted men in Rest Camp about 1 mile from place of landing. Reported to O.C., M.T. Depot. Men were inoculated.	
ROUEN.	23.	—	Dismounted M.T. Vehicles, and parked by the Rest Camp. Started to draw additional stores.	
"	24.	—	Continued drawing stores, and cleaning cars for Inspection. Sunday morning Inspection personnel and cars.	
"	25.	4 p.m.	Left ROUEN for ABBEVILLE, via Neufchatel	
NEUFCHATEL	"	6.30 p.m.	Arrived here. Passed through town, and parked on its verge. Stayed the night. Self, N.C.O's and men slept in cars and lorries.	R. Blair O.C. R.A.W.

WAR DIARY
or
INTELLIGENCE SUMMARY.

(Erase heading not required.)

Army Form C. 2118.

Instructions regarding War Diaries and Intelligence Summaries are contained in F. S. Regs., Part II. and the Staff Manual respectively. Title pages will be prepared in manuscript.

Place	Date	Hour	Summary of Events and Information	Remarks and references to Appendices
NEUFCHATEL	July 26	7am	Left with convoy for ABBEVILLE. Passed 268 Bo, arriving	
ABBEVILLE	" 26	1.30 p.m.	at Abbeville at 1 p.m. Reported to O.B., advanced M.T. Depot, who handed me further orders to proceed at once with motor Ambulances for ST OMER; workshop, store lorry, and eight	
ST OMER	" 26	8.30 p.m.	lorry to ST MARTIN. Reached ST OMER 8.30 p.m. Having left store lorry 15 miles behind, with workshop and light lorry towing it in, these	
ST MARTIN	27 9 am		three vehicles arrived at midnight. Remained in St Omer rest of night with complete convoy. Reported to R.A.R.M.S., 20th Division's A.Q.t. at LUMBRES, who ordered me to remove complete convoy to field in ST MARTIN on the following day.	
ST OMER	27	9.30 a.m.	Reported to D.D.M.S., G.H.Q. who enquired of the whereabouts of my Convoy. I informed him of the instructions received from the D.A.Q.M.S., XXth Division re my move on this day to St Martin. He asked me to report to him on the following day.	R.B.L Lt O.C. Q.A.W.
ST OMER "	10.30 a.m.		M.T. Vehicles inspected by Major Hutchinson. arm. left ~~proved~~ with 16 convoy for ST MARTIN.	

Army Form C. 2118.

WAR DIARY
or
INTELLIGENCE SUMMARY.
(Erase heading not required.)

Instructions regarding War Diaries and Intelligence Summaries are contained in F. S. Regs., Part II. and the Staff Manual respectively. Title pages will be prepared in manuscript.

Place	Date	Hour	Summary of Events and Information	Remarks and references to Appendices
ST. MARTIN	JULY 27	10.30 p.m.	Parked in field.	
	28	2 am	Received orders to despatch an Ambulance for duty to the 4th. Ambulance of the Division.	
	29		Carried on with Repairs	
	30			
MERRIS.	31	11 am	Left for ST. MARTIN for Merris. Parked in field, 500 yds. from Church.	
	AUG. 1		Carried on with Repairs, making alterations to Ford Ambs.	R.B.L. C.C.O.W.
	2			
	3			
	4			
	5			
	6			
	7			
	8			
	9			
	10			
	11			
	12			
	13			
	14			

Army Form C. 2118.

WAR DIARY
or
INTELLIGENCE SUMMARY.
(Erase heading not required.)

Place	Date	Hour	Summary of Events and Information	Remarks and references to Appendices
MERRIS	Aug 16	—	No remarks	
	17		"	
	18		"	
	19		"	
	20		"	
	21		"	
	22		"	
	23		"	
	24		"	
ESTAIRES	25	5pm	Moved from Merris to Estaires, arriving there 8 p.m. Parked and billeted, 9.25 c.	
	26		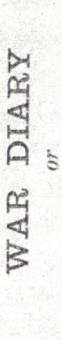 Started to repair machinery in factory for 20th Div, Baths, and carried on with repairs to Amb. Cars.	
	27			
	28			
	29			
	30			
	31			
	SEPT 1–5		Tested and ran Baths machinery successfully and carried on Amb. Car repairs.	R.B.L ir O.C. O.K.W.
	6			
	7			

Army Form C. 2118.

WAR DIARY
or
INTELLIGENCE SUMMARY.
(Erase heading not required.)

R. B. E. Li:-
O.C. XX AW.

Place	Date	Hour	Summary of Events and Information	Remarks and references to Appendices
ESTAIRES	SEPT. 6,9,10,13,14,15,17,18,19,20,21,22,23,24,25,27,28,29,30 OCT. 1,2,3,4,5,6,7,8		Carried on with repairs to Amb. cars. No Remarks. "	

Army Form C. 2118.

Instructions regarding War Diaries and Intelligence Summaries are contained in F. S. Regs., Part II. and the Staff Manual respectively. Title pages will be prepared in manuscript.

WAR DIARY
or
INTELLIGENCE SUMMARY.
(Erase heading not required.)

Place	Date	Hour	Summary of Events and Information	Remarks and references to Appendices
ESTAIRES	Oct.			
	10			
	11			
	12			
	13			
	14			
	15			
	16			
	17			
	18			
	19		Went on leave to England. Lt. Done, R.A.M.C., sanitary section 38nd., taking charge of my Unit for the term of my absence.	
	20			
	21			
	22			
	23			
	24			
	25		- No remarks.	
	26			
	27			
	28			
	29		Arrived back from leave, taking over command of the Unit from Lt. Done, R.A.M.C.	R. Bro. L. OC. D.KW.
	30		" No remarks	
	31		"	

Army Form C. 2118.

WAR DIARY
or
INTELLIGENCE SUMMARY.
(Erase heading not required.)

Instructions regarding War Diaries and Intelligence Summaries are contained in F. S. Regs., Part II. and the Staff Manual respectively. Title pages will be prepared in manuscript.

R.B.Les-
O.C.D.A.W.

Place	Date	Hour	Summary of Events and Information	Remarks and references to Appendices
ESTAIRES	Nov. 1		Carried on with Amb. Repairs. No remarks.	
	2		"	
	3		"	
	4		"	
	5		"	
	6		"	
	7		"	
	8		"	
	9		"	
	10		"	
	11		"	
	12		"	
	13		"	
	14		"	
	15		"	
	16		"	
	17		"	
	18		"	
	19		"	
	20		"	
	21		"	
	22		"	
	23		"	
	24		"	
	25		"	
	26		"	
	27		"	
	28		"	
	29		"	
	30		"	

Army Form C. 2118.

WAR DIARY
or
INTELLIGENCE SUMMARY.
(Erase heading not required.)

Instructions regarding War Diaries and Intelligence Summaries are contained in F. S. Regs., Part II. and the Staff Manual respectively. Title pages will be prepared in manuscript.

Place	Date	Hour	Summary of Events and Information	Remarks and references to Appendices
ESTAIRES.	DEC. 1		Carried on with Amb. Repairs. No remarks.	
	2		" "	
	3		" "	
	4		" "	
	5		" "	
	6		" "	
	7		" "	
	8		" "	
	9		" "	
	10		" "	
	11		" "	
	12		" "	
	13		" "	
	14		" "	
	15		" "	
	16		" "	
	17		" "	
	18		" "	
	19		" "	
	20		" "	
	21		" "	
	22		" "	
	23		" "	
	24		" "	
	25		" "	
	26		" "	
	27		" "	
	28		" "	
	29		" "	
	30		" "	
	31		" "	

R.B-bLt
GE.TAW

WAR DIARY

INTELLIGENCE SUMMARY.

(Erase heading not required.)

Army Form C. 2118.

Place	Date	Hour	Summary of Events and Information	Remarks and references to Appendices
ESTAIRES	1/16	11.0.A.M. 6.0.p.m.	Attended Court of Inquiry Ordered by A.D.M.S. to hear evidence from 1st & 2nd Drivers of Ford Amb. Car. No. 7/0. recently damaged in a collision with a Singer Car driven by Lt. Mitchell. It seems from the evidence that the Driver of the Singer Car was entirely in the wrong. The weather has been cold and wet.	R.B.C.
		6.0 P.M.	Reported that all low lamps have been fitted to Amb Cars, to A.D.M.S.	R.B.C.
"	2/16	8.0.a.m. 11.0.a.m.	Weather wet but rather warmer than yesterday. Continuous firing of heavy guns heard. Have received Secret Orders about the move back of the 20th Div. for rest and training and the forward movement into E staires of the 8th Div during next week. My Unit is remaining also the 160th and 61st Field Ambulances. A/c Cpl Wallace. E.C. arrived back from leave in England.	R.B.C. R.B.C.
"	3/16	7.0 p.m.	No remarks.	R.B.C. C.C.D.K.W.

WAR DIARY or INTELLIGENCE SUMMARY.

Army Form C. 2118.

Place	Date	Hour	Summary of Events and Information	Remarks and references to Appendices
ESTAIRES	JAN. 14/16	—	No remarks.	
	15			
	16			
	17			
	18			
	19			
	20			
	21			
	22			
	23			
	24			
	25			
	26		In preparation for move evacuated Touring car and Ford Amb, to 3rd A.T.C. Report	
			Received moving orders from A.D.M.S., to move to Hazebrouck on the 27th.	shop.
HAZEBROUCK	27	3pm	left ESTAIRES, 3 p.m., arriving HAZEBROUCK 6 p.m.	
		6pm	Parked and opened up Workshop, Sheet 36a, 1:40,000 D 36.	
	27	7pm	Reported to Town Mayor, obtaining through him billets for self,	R. B.L.
			N.C.O's and men, and an office.	O.C. D.A.W.

Army Form C. 2118.

WAR DIARY
or
INTELLIGENCE SUMMARY.
(Erase heading not required.)

Instructions regarding War Diaries and Intelligence Summaries are contained in F. S. Regs., Part II. and the Staff Manual respectively. Title pages will be prepared in manuscript.

Place	Date	Hour	Summary of Events and Information	Remarks and references to Appendices
HAZEBROUCK	JAN. 28	—	Received Orders from A.D.O. to draw rations from 20th Div. Amm. Sub. Park. Carried out repairs under very awkward conditions, there being no covering or shelter whatever.	R.B.E. O.C. XX.A.W.
	29	—	Am finding it very unsatisfactory to be so far away from the A.D. Amn's and A. Gen. of the Division	
	30	—	} no remarks.	
	31	—		

WAR DIARIES OF THE 20th Divisional Field Ambulance

Workshop Unit- Volumes 2 and 3.

FEBRUARY and March 1916

COMMITTEE FOR THE
MEDICAL HISTORY OF THE WAR

Date

2o Jawu.
vols 2, 3

WAR DIARY 20th DIV. AMBce WORKSHOP

INTELLIGENCE SUMMARY.

(Erase heading not required.)

Place	Date	Hour	Summary of Events and Information	Remarks and references to Appendices
HAZE-BROUCK	Feb. 1	—	No remarks	R.B.C.
	2	—	do.	R.B.C.
	3	—	Received orders to move to ESQUELBECQUE.	R.B.C
	4	—	Packed up and ready to move. Having orders cancelled. Reported to A.D.M.S. the undesirability of being so far away from Amb. Cars, which need increasing attention.	
	5	"	Carried in repairs to cars.	R.B.C.
	6	"	Received orders to move to ESQUELBECQUE on the 7th.	R.B.C.
	7	7am	Moved to ESQUELBECQUE, arrp. at 7am with advance party, at about 21.6.8.5.0.	R.B.C.
	7	3pm	Moved H.Q. mill hand-lorries.	R.B.C.
ESQUEL-BECQUE	7	4pm	A.D.S. Equipment was transported to A.D.M.S., and "D" office, and arrived 4d. Ambs.	R.B.G.
	4			R.B.G.

WAR DIARY 20th Div: Amb. Workshop.

INTELLIGENCE SUMMARY.

Army Form C. 2118.

Instructions regarding War Diaries and Intelligence Summaries are contained in F.S. Regs., Part II. and the Staff Manual respectively. Title pages will be prepared in manuscript.

(Erase heading not required.)

Place	Date	Hour	Summary of Events and Information	Remarks and references to Appendices
ESQUEL- BECQUE	Feb 8		On working order, repairing Amb. Cars.	R.B.C.
	9		Lieut. R. Balfour-Slade left for Boulogne for training. Lt. D.S. Hodge, Div. Supp. Col., taking over command.	R.B.C. R.B.C.
	10			R.B.C.
	11		Received orders to move, and ordered 141st Div. Amb. Workshops Lieut.	R.B.C.
	12		Packed up ready for move.	R.B.C.
	13	7 am	Left Esquelbecq, proceeding via Cassel, Abeele and Poperinghe to St Jean-der-Biezen.	R.B.C.
ST. JEAN nr. BURGO	13	10.50 am	Arr. ST. JEAN-DER BIEZEN. Unpacked and started repairs at once.	R.B.C.
	14		Carried on with repairs to Amb. Cars.	R.B.C.
	15		" " " "	R.B.C.
	16		" " " "	R.B.C.
	17		" " " "	R.B.C.
	18		" " " "	R.B.C.
	19		" " " "	R.B.C.
	20		" " " "	R.B.C.

Army Form C. 2118.

WAR DIARY
or
INTELLIGENCE SUMMARY. 20th. Div. Amb. Workshop.

(Erase heading not required.)

Instructions regarding War Diaries and Intelligence Summaries are contained in F. S. Regs., Part II. and the Staff Manual respectively. Title pages will be prepared in manuscript.

Place	Date	Hour	Summary of Events and Information	Remarks and references to Appendices
ST JEAN	11 Au		Party (20 ant) sent to Tire Rues. Rest Then fitted. Received moving Orders.	R B C.
TER				
RIERZIN	23 Mar		morning orders cancelled.	R.B.C.
	23.	—	Lie. R. Balfour-Clarke rejoined Units on completion of period of training.	R.B.C.
	24		}	R.B.C.
	25		} with	
	26		}	R.B.C.
	27		} Engaged in Repairs to Ambulance Cars.	
	28			
	29			

R. Balfour-Clarke
Lt.
O.C. 20th Div. Amb. Workshops.

Army Form C. 2118.

WAR DIARY 20th Div'l. Amb. Workshop

INTELLIGENCE SUMMARY
(Erase heading not required.)

Instructions regarding War Diaries and Intelligence Summaries are contained in F. S. Regs., Part II. and the Staff Manual respectively. Title pages will be prepared in manuscript.

Place	Date	Hour	Summary of Events and Information	Remarks and references to Appendices
ST. JAN TER.	MARCH 1 2 3		} Carried on Ambulance Repairs.	R.B.C.
BIERZEN	4	9.30 Am.	Painting light lorry, departed at 9.30 p.m. to A.28a 5.6 for the purpose of towing in Talbot of 2nd Fd. Amb.	R.B.C.
	5 6 7 8 9 10 11 12 13 14		} Carried on Repairs to Ambulance Cars, and erection of suitable sheds for repairing cars in wet weather.	R.B.C.
	15		Forwarded to 3rd A.T.C. Repair shop, Frame no. 17116, Engine no. 21549 Douglas Motor bicycle.	R.B.C.
	16 17 18		} Carried on repairs to Ambul. cars.	R.B.C.

2353 Wt. W2514/1454 700,000 5/15 D. D. & L. A.D.S.S./Forms/C. 2118.

Army Form C. 2118.

WAR DIARY

INTELLIGENCE SUMMARY. 20th Divl. Amb. Workshop.

(Erase heading not required.)

Instructions regarding War Diaries and Intelligence Summaries are contained in F. S. Regs., Part II. and the Staff Manual respectively. Title pages will be prepared in manuscript.

Place	Date	Hour	Summary of Events and Information	Remarks and references to Appendices
STTAN-TER-BIERZEN	MARCH 19 20 21 22	- - - -	Continued repairs and renewals to Ambulances.	RBC
	23	-	Qr. Mr. Sergt. White proceeded on leave to U.K., Capt. Dore, Sanitary Section 33, taking over command.	RBC RBC RBC
	24 25	" "	" No remarks.	
	26	"	Received four new "Triumph" Motor Cycles to bring up War Establishment	RBC
	27 28 29	" " "	} No remarks	RBC
	30	-	Received Douglas M/C to complete War Establishment, Lt. R. W. Scott Clarke returned from leave to U.K., Capt. Dore relinquishing command.	RBC
	31	-	Received R.O., No. 56, by Col. E.W. Haytel, A.D.M.S., 20th Division, that 20th Divl. Amb. Workshop officially abolished, and personnel and vehicles, with the exception of Touring Car, a Light Lorry, and their drivers transferred to 20 DE Divisional Supp. Col. P.T.O.	RBC

R. Balfour Clarke.
O.C. 20th Div. Amb. Workshop.

www.ingramcontent.com/pod-product-compliance
Lightning Source LLC
Chambersburg PA
CBHW081250170426
43191CB00037B/2104